The Burro's Land

by Adela Chavez
illustrated by George Ulrich

Printed in the United States of America

ISBN 0-15-317317-3 – The Burro's Land

Ordering Options
ISBN 0-15-318661-5 (Package of 5)
ISBN 0-15-316987-7 (Grade 3 Package)

2 3 4 5 6 7 8 9 10 179 02 01 00

The burro had wandered the desert her whole life. She knew the warm feel of sun on her coat. She knew where there was water. When she was hungry, she looked for the places where the desert growth was ample and ate there.

The burro shunned people. There were not many, but the burro stayed away from them. When she saw a windmill, she knew people were close by. When she saw furrows, she knew they meant farms and did not go near.

Then a young miner found her. He was hunting for a gold mine he had heard about that was high in the California mountains. He saw the burro, and his eyes shone. Here was the help he needed!

Slowly he crept up behind the burro. He threw a rope around her neck. The burro struggled.

"Whoa, girl," the miner said. He patted the burro. "You'll be all right."

At first, the burro did not trust the miner. He had stolen her cherished freedom, after all.

The man spoke softly to her. He petted her and fed her. Sometimes he gave her treats—carrots and greens. Finally, the burro grew to trust the man.

"I'm going to name you Lightning," the man told her one day. "You still have some wildness in you, don't you?"

Together they searched for gold. They traveled far from the neat furrows and windmills where people lived. They went deep into the mountains, where, one day, the man found gold.

"Lightning, old girl," the miner said, "this is it! There is gold here! Yippee!" The man threw his hat into the air.

For months, the man worked to dig out the gold. The burro carried load after load down the mountain. The man was always kind. There was always an ample supply of food.

4

After about a year, the miner found less and less gold. One day he patted the burro's head and said, "Well, old girl, it's time for me to go back home. I think we've done all we can here."

The miner packed up his things and took the burro to the closest farm. He offered her to the family. They were happy to have such a useful animal to help with their work.

The miner took his packs off the burro. "Good luck, Lightning," he said, his voice shaking. "I've cherished you. You have been a good friend. I couldn't have done it without you. Now it's time for me to go back to the city. You will be happy and cared for here."

At first, the burro was afraid of the family's children. She was unsure of what they would do. She had grown used to life with only the man. Eventually, however, the burro became used to her new home. She lived a long and happy life.

For many years, packs of burros lived as Lightning had before she met the man. They shunned people. They ate the thick desert growth.

It was a fine life. Each herd grew larger over time as young were born. The young burros would run for miles in the open desert just for the fun of it. They loved to feel the wind in their manes.

The burros lived well, but as the herds grew larger, their lands got smaller.

More people moved to this part of the desert. There was less and less land for the burros. The herds began to see more farms and more roads.

Lately men had been coming in trucks with ropes to catch the burros. When the burros saw these men, they scattered in alarm. Sometimes, though, the men caught a burro and put it in the truck.

8

One day, a young burro heard a truck coming up behind her. Wildly, she ran. The truck grew nearer.

"Come on, girl," she heard a man say. "Calm down. Let me get you." The burro felt a rope on her neck. It jerked her backward.

"That's it," the man said. The burro twisted wildly.

The burro soon found herself in a strange place. Fences were on all sides. Other burros shared a small space with her. The young burro was scared.

By the fence, a family watched. "Oh, Mommy, can't we get one?" said a girl.

"I don't think so," her mother said. "These burros are wild. They don't know anything about people."

"They make gentle pets," said a voice nearby. "I work here. These burros are great for families. They train well. They don't stay wild."

"That one is good looking," the father said, pointing to the young burro.

"Please, Daddy?" the girl said. The parents looked at each other.

"Well, we had talked about a horse, but I like that one, too," the mother said. She thought a minute longer. "Sure. Why not?"

"Thank you so much!" the girl shouted.

The young burro had a hard time at first.
Everything was so strange. But the food was
plentiful, and the family was kind.

"What shall we call her?" the mother asked.

"Well, she's wild," the girl said. "What about
Wild One?"

"What about Lightning?" asked the father.
"Have you seen her run?"

"I like that," the girl decided. She put her
arms around the burro's neck and gave her a
carrot. "Lightning, we'll be friends forever."

More of the Burro's Story

On a sheet of paper, write a book review for your friends. Tell what you liked most and least about the story. Tell whether you think your friends should read the book, too. Use a chart like the one below to organize your thoughts.

The Burro's Land	
liked most	**liked least**

School-Home Connection Listen as your child reads the story aloud. Ask your child to describe how a wild animal's life changes when it lives with people.

TAKE-HOME BOOK
Journeys of Wonder
Use with "Alejandro's Gift."